Rookie Cookie Cookbook

Rookie Cookie Cookbook

Betty Debman

Gramercy Books
New York

This 2000 edition is published by Gramercy Books™,
an imprint of Random House Value Publishing, Inc.,
280 Park Avenue, New York, New York 10017,
by arrangement with Andrews McMeel Publishing.

Gramercy Books™ and design are trademarks of
Random House Value Publishing, Inc.

Random House
New York • Toronto • London • Sydney • Auckland
http://www.randomhouse.com/

Printed and bound in the United States of America

A CIP catalog record for this book is available from the Library of Congress.

ISBN 0-517-16246-6

8 7 6 5 4 3 2 1

CONTENTS

RECIPE FOR
A GOOD COOK

- 1 adult standing by when you use a knife, blender, hot range, or oven.
- 2 clean hands.
- 1 apron tied around the waist.
- A well-read recipe and everything ready to mix.
- Pots and pans with handles turned to the back of the range so you can't knock them off.
- 2 dry pot holders.
- A cooking time that suits your parent.
- 1 clean kitchen after you have finished.
- 1 or more eaters to tell you and all your friends what a good cook you are.

RECIPE FOR A GOOD MICROWAVE COOK

- An adult standing by when you use the microwave oven.
- 1 smart finger that punches the right buttons when setting the time.
- 2 smart hands that, when they remove the lid, always point it away from the body. In this way, the steam goes the other way.
- 2 pot holders to use when taking food out of the oven.
- A roll of plastic wrap to use to cover foods so they won't splatter. Always turn back a corner when using it as a lid. This allows some of the steam to escape.
- Dishes that are microwave-safe.
- A smart operator who never turns on the oven when it is empty.
- A roll of paper towels to use when cleaning oven or covering some foods. Use the type recommended for microwave ovens.

GOOD COOKS READ AND UNDERSTAND THE RECIPE WELL BEFORE THEY START.

MEASURING

Careful measuring is an important step in cooking.

When you measure dry things such as flour, sugar, or spices, completely fill the cup or spoon. Level it off with a knife.

When measuring margarine or butter, pack the cup or spoon and level off with a knife, too.

For liquids, it is handy to use a clear measuring cup with the measurements written on the sides.

Some useful measures follow:

"Pinch" or "Dash" = less than ⅛ teaspoon

3 teaspoons = 1 tablespoon

16 tablespoons = 1 cup

1 cup = 8 fluid ounces

2 cups = 1 pint

2 pints = 1 quart

4 quarts = 1 gallon

ONE CUP IS EQUAL TO 8 FLUID OUNCES!

UTENSILS

 casserole

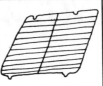 wire rack

 mixing bowls

 square baking pan

 colander

double boiler

muffin pan

rolling pin

fork

loaf pan

strainer

tongs

baking pan

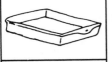 pancake turner

 saucepan

 layer cake pan

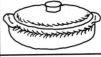 baking dish

 spatula

 skillet

 slotted spoon

 vegetable brush

 vegetable parer

 kitchen shears

 potato masher

 egg beater

COOKING WORDS

Blend: mix two or more items until smooth.

Broil: cook directly under heating coil in the oven.

Coat: cover completely with thin layer.

Core: remove middle and seeds from fruit or vegetable.

Cream: beat or mix two or more ingredients together until smooth and creamy.

Cube: cut into small squares.

Dot: scatter bits of food such as butter or cheese on top of the food being cooked.

Grate: cut food into small pieces by rubbing against grater.

Grease: rub the cooking surface of a pan with butter or margarine to keep food from sticking.

Knead: work dough with hands by pulling, pressing, and twisting.

Preheat: heat oven to temperature you want before putting food in.

Simmer: heat liquid.

THESE ARE A FEW WORDS TO COOK BY!

CORN MEAL

HOW TO SET THE TABLE

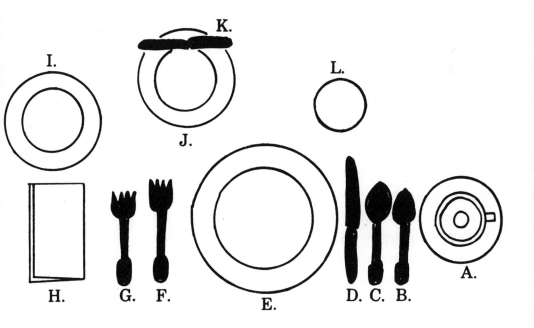

A. Cup and saucer
B. Spoon
C. Dessert spoon
D. Knife
E. Dinner plate
F. Fork

G. Salad fork
H. Napkin
I. Salad plate
J. Bread and butter
K. Butter knife
L. Glass

The above setting might use more plates and silver than you wish to use.

If so, use the above plan, but leave out what you do not use.

If you are asked to serve, remember—serve to the left; take away dishes from the right.

TABLE MANNERS

- Offer to seat the older people and girls.
- Chew with your mouth closed. Try to clean your plate.
- Take soup from the side of the spoon.
- Keep your napkin in your lap. When you have finished, wait for the hostess to put her napkin on the table. Then you can put yours down (slightly folded) on the left side of your plate.
- Keep your elbows off the table.
- Be polite about passing things. A pitcher is passed with the handle toward the person getting it.
- Talk about pleasant subjects.
- Do not blow on your food to cool it.
- If you are served something you don't like, just leave it on your plate. Don't comment on it.
- If your hostess offers you a food you don't like, a simple "No, thank you" will do.
- Ask to be excused before leaving the table.
- Say how much you enjoyed the meal.
- Offer to help with the dishes.

Rookie
Cookie...
that little
deer in the
kitchen.

Debnam

INTRODUCING ROOKIE COOKIE
AND THE MINI PAGE GANG!

BEAN DIP

You'll need:
1 can (10 oz.) bean with bacon soup
1 cup chili sauce
1 teaspoon onion, minced
1 teaspoon Worcestershire sauce

What to do:
1. Place all ingredients in a blender.
2. Blend until smooth.
3. Serve with your favorite crackers or chips.

Makes about 1½ cups.

NO-COOK SNACKS

Yogurt and Granola
Mix 1 cup of your favorite yogurt with ¼ cup granola cereal.

Orange Sundae
Pour thawed orange juice concentrate over a scoop of vanilla ice cream.

Meat and Cheese
Layer sliced meat and cheese on bread or crackers. For fun, cut bread into unusual shapes using cookie cutters.

Celery Stuffers
Stuff celery with peanut butter, cream cheese, or pimento cheese.

Shish Kebabs
Stick toothpicks through pieces of cheese, ham, hot dogs, Vienna sausages, and pineapple to make tiny shish kebabs.

PIZZA ROUNDS

You'll need:
1 cup Cheddar cheese, grated
⅔ cup ready-made spaghetti or pizza sauce
7 to 9 slices of bread
3 tablespoons margarine, melted

What to do:
1. Mix sauce and cheese in a bowl.
2. Trim crusts from bread. Spread sauce and cheese on bread.
3. Roll up each slice and fasten with a toothpick.
4. Place bread on a cookie sheet. Brush with margarine. Refrigerate 15 minutes.
5. Bake in a preheated 400°F oven for 15 minutes.

MAMMA MIA!

EGGS

BREAKFAST CASSEROLE

You'll need:
  30 saltine crackers, crushed
  2 cups Cheddar cheese, grated
  6 eggs
  1 stick margarine, melted
  2 cups milk
  ½ cup bacon bits

What to do:
  1. Put crackers in a greased 12x8-inch baking dish.
  2. Combine remaining ingredients in a bowl and mix well.
  3. Pour mixture over crackers. Bake in a preheated 400°F oven for 20 minutes or until done.
Serves 6.

BULL'S-EYE EGGS

You'll need:
1 slice bread per serving
1 egg per serving
1 tablespoon margarine per serving

What to do:
1. Using a glass, cut a hole in each slice of bread.
2. Melt margarine in a frying pan over medium heat. Brown bread on both sides.
3. Put bread in a shallow, greased baking dish. Break an egg in each hole. Put a dab of butter on each egg.
4. Bake in a preheated 300°F oven for about 10 minutes or until eggs are hard.

CREAMED EGG TOPPING

This is a good recipe to use if guests pop in when you are not expecting them!

You'll need:
 4 eggs
 1 can (10 oz.) cream of mushroom soup
 ½ teaspoon soy sauce
 ¼ teaspoon Worcestershire sauce

What to do:
 1. Hard-boil eggs and slice them.
 2. In a saucepan, mix eggs, cream of mushroom soup, soy sauce, and Worcestershire sauce.
 3. Heat mixture on low heat. Be careful not to boil.
 4. Serve on rice, toast, or toasted English muffin.
Serves 4.

MEXICAN EGGS

You'll need:
  1 can (8 oz.) tomato sauce
  ½ teaspoon chili powder
  6 eggs
  ½ cup Cheddar cheese, grated
  Tortilla chips, crushed

What to do:
1. In a small bowl combine tomato sauce and chili powder. Mix well. Pour into a 9-inch pie pan.
2. Break eggs on top of sauce, spacing them evenly. Do not stir.
3. Bake in a preheated 350°F oven for 30 minutes.
4. Remove from oven and sprinkle with cheese.
5. For each serving, put a handful of chips in a bowl. Top with an egg and some of the sauce.

Serves 6.

SANDWICHES AND SPREADS

APPLE SALAD SANDWICH

You'll need:
   1 apple, peeled and finely diced
   ⅓ cup raisins
   ⅓ cup celery, chopped
   ⅓ cup mayonnaise
   1 cup Cheddar cheese, grated

What to do:
   1. Combine all ingredients and mix well.
   2. Spread between bread to make sandwiches.
Serves 4.

SAY CHEESE!

GRATE
GRATE
GRATE

RAISINS

MAYONNA

CHEESY CUCUMBER SANDWICH

You'll need:
  1 package (3-oz.) cream cheese
  1 teaspoon milk
  Onion salt
  Garlic salt
  1 cucumber, peeled and thinly sliced
  6 slices bread

What to do:
  1. Mix cream cheese with milk to soften.
  2. Season with onion and garlic salts to taste.
  3. Spread cream cheese mixture on bread slices. Top with cucumber slices.
Makes 3 sandwiches.

CHICKEN IN A BUN

You'll need:
2 cups cooked chicken, diced
½ cup celery, diced
2 tablespoons onion, chopped
½ cup cheese, grated
2 hard-cooked eggs, chopped
¾ cup mayonnaise
Salt and pepper
Butter or margarine
6 hamburger buns

What to do:
1. Combine chicken, celery, onion, cheese, eggs, and mayonnaise. Add salt and pepper to taste.
2. Butter buns and fill with mixture.
3. Wrap each bun in aluminum foil. Heat in a preheated 400°F oven for 15 to 20 minutes.

Serves 6.

EGG SALAD SANDWICH

You'll need:
   3 hard-cooked eggs
   1 tablespoon pickle relish
   3 tablespoons mayonnaise
   6 slices bread

What to do:
   1. Peel eggs. Mash them with a fork.
   2. Add pickle relish and mayonnaise.
   3. Spread on bread for sandwiches.
Serves 3.

GREAT LUNCH!

PITA BREAD
TURKEY SANDWICH

You'll need:
2 cups cooked turkey, diced
½ cup celery, diced
¼ cup onion, chopped
2 hard-cooked eggs, chopped
1 tablespoon lemon juice
½ teaspoon salt
¼ teaspoon pepper
¾ cup mayonnaise
4 pieces of pita bread

What to do:
1. Combine all ingredients and mix well.
2. Stuff mixture inside pita bread to serve.
Serves 4.

REUBEN SANDWICH

You'll need:
   8 slices rye bread
   Swiss cheese slices
   Sauerkraut
   Corned beef slices
   Margarine

What to do:
   1. Fill 4 slices of bread with cheese, sauerkraut, and corned beef.
   2. Top with remaining slices of bread.
   3. Spread margarine on outside of each sandwich.
   4. Place each sandwich in a skillet and brown slightly on each side.
Makes 4 sandwiches.

SALAD IN A SANDWICH

You'll need:
  1 small head of lettuce
  1 carrot, sliced
  1 tomato, chopped
  1 small onion, chopped
  1 cucumber, sliced
  4 pieces of pita bread
  Your favorite salad dressing

What to do:
  1. Tear lettuce into small pieces and mix with vegetables.
  2. Cut pita bread in half and stuff pockets with salad mixture.
  3. Pour a little salad dressing into each pocket.
Makes 4 servings.

FUN TO FIX!

GOOD TO EAT!

SANDWICH SWITCH-A-ROOS

- In place of white bread, try crackers, bagels, corn or bran muffins, pita bread, English muffins, taco shells, raisin bread, grain bread, tortillas, or croissant rolls.

- In place of lettuce, try cucumber slices, pickles, cabbage, zucchini slices, alfalfa sprouts, green pepper strips, or bean sprouts.

- In place of jelly with your peanut butter sandwich, try raisins, sliced bananas, sliced apples, grated carrots, or bacon bits.

SEABURGERS

You'll need:
 1 can (6½ oz.) tuna, drained
 ¼ cup mayonnaise
 ¼ cup catsup
 ¾ cup American cheese, grated
 6 hamburger buns

What to do:
 1. Combine tuna, mayonnaise, catsup, and cheese in a bowl and mix well.
 2. Spoon into hamburger buns.
 3. Wrap each bun in foil. Heat in a preheated 350°F oven for 15 minutes. If you wish, add pickle relish before serving.
Serves 6.

DOGGONE SOUP

You'll need:
3 hot dogs, thinly sliced
1 can (10 oz.) bean with bacon soup
1 soup can milk

What to do:
1. Place all ingredients in a pot.
2. Cook over medium heat until warm. Stir often.
Serves 3.

HEARTY BEEF AND VEGETABLE SOUP

You'll need:
½ pound lean ground beef
1 medium onion, chopped
1 can (28 oz.) stewed tomatoes
1 cup water
1 can (15 oz.) red kidney beans
2 medium carrots, sliced
½ medium head of cabbage, cut into chunks
¼ cup macaroni
1 chicken bouillon cube
1 teaspoon basil
Dash of pepper

What to do:
1. Brown beef and onion in a large pot.
2. Stir in all other ingredients.
3. Cook over medium heat until macaroni and vegetables are soft, about 20 minutes.

Serves 8.

COME IN AND WARM UP!

CASSEROLES AND VEGETABLES

BAKED BEANS

You'll need:
1 can (16 oz.) pork and beans
1 medium onion, chopped
1 medium green pepper, chopped
½ cup brown sugar
1 teaspoon mustard
3 slices bacon

What to do:
1. Place all ingredients except bacon in a casserole dish. Mix well.
2. Top with bacon.
3. Bake in a preheated 325°F oven for 45 minutes.

Serves 4.

CASSEROLES ARE GOOD FILLER-UPPERS!

I LOVE BAKED BEANS!

BAKED TOMATOES

You'll need:
2 cups soda cracker crumbs
1 cup Cheddar cheese, grated
1 cup onion, chopped
3 cups canned tomatoes with juice
1 tablespoon butter

What to do:
1. Combine cracker crumbs, cheese, and onion. Mix well.
2. Place in a greased casserole dish.
3. Pour tomatoes over cracker mixture.
4. Dot with butter. Bake in a preheated 350°F oven for 30 minutes.

Serves 6.

TOMATOES ARE EASY TO GROW!

CHEESE CASSEROLE

You'll need:
  12 slices bread
  ½ stick butter or margarine
  5 cups American cheese, grated
  6 eggs, slightly beaten
  1 teaspoon salt
  2 cans (12 oz.) evaporated milk
  1½ cups water

What to do:
  1. Butter bread and cut each slice into four parts.
  2. Alternate layers of bread and cheese in a large, shallow baking dish ending with a layer of cheese on top.
  3. Mix eggs, salt, milk, and water in a bowl. Pour in casserole dish.
  4. Let sit 3 hours. Bake in a preheated 325°F oven for 35 minutes.
Serves about 12

SERVES 12, OR 6 OF US TWICE!

CORN PUDDING

You'll need:
- 2 eggs, beaten
- 1 tablespoon all-purpose flour
- 3 tablespoons butter, melted
- ⅓ cup sugar
- 1 cup milk
- 1 tablespoon vanilla
- ½ teaspoon salt
- 1 can (17 oz.) corn, drained

What to do:
1. In bowl, combine all ingredients except corn. Mix well.
2. Stir corn into mixture.
3. Pour into a greased casserole dish. Bake in a pre-heated 400°F oven for 40 minutes.

Serves 6 to 8.

MACARONI PIE

You'll need:
½ pound macaroni, cooked
1½ tablespoons butter
1½ cups Cheddar cheese, grated
½ teaspoon dry mustard
Pepper
3 eggs, beaten
1½ cups milk

What to do:
1. In a bowl, combine macaroni, butter, 1 cup of cheese, and mustard. Add pepper to taste. Stir well.
2. Add eggs and milk. Stir well.
3. Put in a greased casserole. Top with remaining cheese. Bake in a preheated 350°F oven for 40 minutes.
Serves 6.

POTATO CASSEROLE

You'll need:

   1 bag (2 pound) frozen hash brown potatoes, thawed
   1/4 cup margarine, melted
   1 can (10 oz.) cream of mushroom soup
   1/2 cup onion, chopped
   1 cup Cheddar cheese, grated
   1/2 cup potato chips, crushed

What to do:

1. Place hash brown potatoes, margarine, soup, onion, and cheese in a casserole.
2. Sprinkle potato chips on top.
3. Bake in a preheated 350°F oven for 45 minutes.

Serves 6.

SUCCOTASH

You'll need:
  1 can (17 oz.) corn
  1 can (17 oz.) lima beans
  ½ teaspoon salt
  3 tablespoons butter

What to do:
  1. Combine all ingredients in a pot.
  2. Cook over medium heat until warm.
Serves 6.

A WONDERFUL MARRIAGE OF LIMA BEANS AND CORN!

MAIN DISHES

BARBECUE FRANKS

You'll need:
1 tablespoon margarine
¼ cup onion, chopped
1 cup applesauce
½ cup catsup
2 tablespoons mustard
2 tablespoons vinegar
2 tablespoons brown sugar
4 hot dogs, cut into bite-size pieces

What to do:
1. Cook onion in margarine in a saucepan over medium heat until tender.
2. Add remaining ingredients.
3. Simmer 20 minutes.
4. Serve in hot dog or hamburger buns.

Serves 4.

THESE ARE REALLY GOOD!

BEEF AND BISCUITS

You'll need:

1 can (16 oz.) beef stew
1 carrot, sliced
1 can (4 oz.) mushrooms, drained
1 package (8 oz.) refrigerated biscuits

What to do:

1. Combine stew, carrot slices, and mushrooms in a casserole. Mix well.
2. Place biscuits evenly on top.
3. Bake in a preheated 350°F oven for 20 minutes.

Serves 4.

CHILI AND CHEESE BURGERS

You'll need:

1½ pounds ground beef
1 slice bread, torn into crumbs
1 can (10 oz.) Cheddar cheese soup
¼ cup chili sauce
2 teaspoons prepared mustard

What to do:

1. Combine beef, bread crumbs, and ½ can soup. Shape into 6 patties.
2. Place in a baking pan.
3. Combine rest of soup, chili sauce, and mustard. Pour over patties.
4. Cover the baking pan with foil. Bake in a preheated 350°F oven for 45 minutes.

Serves 6.

GREAT AFTER A HARD DAY ON THE TRAIL!

CHICKEN CASSEROLE

You'll need:
2 packages (10 oz.) frozen broccoli
5 cups cooked chicken, diced
2 cans (10 oz.) cream of chicken soup
¾ cup mayonnaise
½ cup milk
2 teaspoons lemon juice
2 cups stuffing mix
1 stick margarine, melted

What to do:
1. Cook broccoli following package directions.
2. Place chicken and broccoli in the bottom of a casserole dish.
3. Combine soup, mayonnaise, milk, and lemon juice. Mix well and pour over chicken and broccoli.
4. Top with stuffing mix. Pour margarine on top.
5. Bake in a preheated 350°F oven for 40 minutes.

Serves 8.

HAPPY MOTHER'S DAY, MOM!

CHICKEN CHOW MEIN

You'll need:
2 cups cooked chicken, diced
1 can (8 oz.) sliced water chestnuts
1 can (10 oz.) cream of mushroom soup
1 tablespoon soy sauce
2 celery stalks, diced
1 can (3 oz.) chow mein noodles

What to do:
1. Combine all ingredients except noodles. Mix well, then gently stir in 1 cup noodles.
2. Place in an 8x8-inch baking dish. Top with remaining noodles.
3. Bake in a preheated 350°F oven for 30 minutes.

Serves 4.

CRUMBY CHICKEN

You'll need:
1 cup bread crumbs
1 cup Parmesan cheese, grated
1 teaspoon garlic salt
Pepper to taste
1 medium frying chicken, cut up
1½ sticks margarine, melted

What to do:
1. Mix together bread crumbs, cheese, garlic salt, and pepper in a bowl.
2. Dip each piece of chicken in margarine then roll in bread crumb mixture.
3. Place in a 13x9-inch baking dish.
4. Bake in a preheated 350°F oven for 1 hour.

Serves 4 to 6.

PIZZA CHICKEN

You'll need:
  6 chicken breasts
  1 jar (15½ oz.) pizza sauce
  1 cup mozzarella cheese, grated

What to do:
  1. Place chicken in a 12x8-inch baking dish.
  2. Bake in a preheated 350°F oven for 30 minutes.
  3. Remove chicken from oven and pour pizza sauce on top. Bake another 30 minutes.
  4. Remove from oven and sprinkle cheese on top. Bake another 5 minutes.
Serves 6.

MOST PEOPLE CAN'T DO THIS! ESPECIALLY WITH MITTS ON!

I LOVE TO MAKE PIZZA!

THIS RECIPE ISN'T A PIZZA, BUT IT'S MADE WITH PIZZA SAUCE.

WOW!

CHICKEN SURPRISE

You'll need:
  12 pieces chicken
  1 envelope (1¼ oz.) onion soup mix
  1 can (10 oz.) cream of mushroom soup
  ½ cup water
  1 can (28 oz.) tomatoes, drained

What to do:
1. Place chicken in a greased 13x9-inch baking dish.
2. Sprinkle onion soup on top.
3. Combine mushroom soup and water. Mix well and pour over chicken.
4. Top with tomatoes.
5. Cover dish with foil. Bake in a preheated 375°F oven for 1 hour.

Serves 6.

SURPRISE!

CHILI DOGS

You'll need:
    1 can (15 oz.) chili with beans
    4 hot dogs
    4 hot dog buns
    ¼ cup green pepper, chopped
    ½ cup Cheddar cheese, grated
    ¼ cup onion, chopped

What to do:
    1. Cook chili and hot dogs following package directions.
    2. Place hot dogs in buns and top with chili.
    3. Top with green pepper, cheese, and onion.
Serves 4.

WARM UP WITH CHILI DOGS!

CHINESE TUNA

You'll need:
   1 can (3 oz.) chow mein noodles
   1 can (10 oz.) cream of mushroom soup
   ¼ cup water
   1 can (8 oz.) water chestnuts, drained
   ½ cup celery, chopped
   1 can (6½ oz.) tuna, drained
   ½ cup onion, chopped

What to do:
   1. Mix ½ can of the noodles with remaining ingredients.
   2. Pour into a casserole. Top with remaining noodles.
   3. Bake in a preheated 325°F oven for 30 minutes.
Serves 4.

FISH AND CHEESE TREAT

You'll need:
1 can (10 oz.) cream of mushroom soup
1 can (10 oz.) Cheddar cheese soup
1 can (6½ oz.) tuna, drained
¼ cup milk
¼ teaspoon oregano
¼ teaspoon Worcestershire sauce
Toast, crackers, or rice

What to do:
1. Combine all ingredients in a saucepan and mix well.
2. Cook over low heat until warm, stirring often.
3. Serve over toast, crackers, or rice.

Serves 6.

HOT DOG PIZZA

You'll need:
  Catsup
  2 English muffins
  1 hot dog, thinly sliced
  ⅓ cup American cheese, grated

What to do:
  1. Spread a little catsup on each muffin half.
  2. Place several hot dog slices on each muffin.
  3. Sprinkle with cheese.
  4. Bake in a preheated 350°F oven 10 minutes or until
     cheese melts.
Serves 2.

MUFFIN PIZZAS

You'll need:
  Tomato sauce
  Pepper and oregano
  English muffins, split in half
  Mozzarella cheese slices
  Parmesan cheese

What to do:
  1. Season tomato sauce with pepper and oregano to taste.
  2. Spread 2 tablespoons sauce on each muffin half.
  3. Top with a slice of mozzarella cheese. Sprinkle with Parmesan cheese.
  4. Place on a baking sheet. Bake in a preheated 350°F oven for 15 to 20 minutes.

ROOKIE'S PIZZA IS FANTASTIC!

PERSONAL PIZZA

You'll need:
1 package of 10 refrigerator biscuits
¼ cup spaghetti or pizza sauce
1 teaspoon oregano
½ cup mozzarella cheese, grated
Toppings of your choice (suggestions: mushrooms, green peppers, olives, sausage)

What to do:
1. Press each biscuit into a 3-inch circle. Place on a greased baking sheet.
2. Combine spaghetti or pizza sauce and oregano in a small bowl.
3. Spread sauce on each biscuit.
4. Top with cheese and any other toppings.
5. Bake in a preheated 400°F oven for 8 minutes.

SPAGHETTI WITH CHEESE

You'll need:
  1 package (8 oz.) spaghetti
  1 jar (16 oz.) pasteurized process cheese spread
  ½ cup bacon bits
  1½ cups skim milk

What to do:
  1. Cook spaghetti following package directions. Place in a 2-quart casserole dish.
  2. Combine cheese spread, milk, and bacon in a saucepan. Cook over low heat until cheese is melted.
  3. Pour cheese mixture over spaghetti. Mix well.
  4. Bake in a preheated 400°F oven for 20 minutes.
Serves 6.

CRUNCHY TURKEY CASSEROLE

You'll need:
   2 cups cooked turkey, diced
   2 cups celery, diced
   ½ cup almonds, toasted
   2 teaspoons onion, chopped
   1 cup mayonnaise
   1 can (10 oz.) cream of celery soup
   1 cup potato chips, crushed

What to do:
   1. Combine turkey, celery, almonds, onion, mayonnaise, and soup. Mix well.
   2. Pour into a 2-quart greased casserole.
   3. Sprinkle with potato chips.
   4. Bake in a preheated 350°F oven for 45 minutes.
Serves 6.

GIVES TURKEY THE ROYAL TREATMENT!

SALADS

CRUNCHY CHICKEN SALAD

You'll need:
   1½ cups cooked chicken, diced
   1 cup celery, diced
   1 cup carrots, shredded
   1 tablespoon pickle relish
   ¾ cup mayonnaise
   1 can (2 oz.) shoestring potatoes

What to do:
   1. Mix chicken, celery, carrots, and pickle relish.
   2. Stir in mayonnaise.
   3. Top with shoestring potatoes.
Serves 4.

EASY TOMATO ASPIC

You'll need:
1 box (3 oz.) lemon gelatin
1 cup hot mixed vegetable juice
1 cup cold mixed vegetable juice
½ cup celery, finely chopped

What to do:
1. Dissolve gelatin in the hot mixed vegetable juice.
2. Stir in the cold mixed vegetable juice and celery.
3. Pour into salad molds. Refrigerate until firm.
4. Unmold onto a lettuce leaf.
Serves 6.

ALMOST TOO PRETTY TO EAT!

SUPER EASY
FRENCH DRESSING

You'll need:
- ¼ cup salad oil
- ¼ cup catsup
- ¼ cup vinegar
- ¼ cup sugar
- ¼ teaspoon garlic salt

What to do:
1. Mix all ingredients in a bottle and shake well.
2. Allow to stand for about an hour before using.

Makes 1 cup.

MIX THIS UP TO TOP
ALL OF YOUR
FAVORITE SALADS!

GUACAMOLE

You'll need:
    1 avocado, ripe
    1 teaspoon onion, minced
    1 teaspoon olive oil
    $\frac{1}{8}$ teaspoon salt
    1 teaspoon lemon juice
    Dash of pepper
    Corn chips

What to do:
    1. Slice avocado in half. Remove pit.
    2. Scoop out pulp. Mash with a fork.
    3. Add remaining ingredients. Mix well.
    Serve with corn chips.
Serves 2.

GUACAMOLE IS THE BEST!

HOT DIGGY DOG SALAD

You'll need:
2 cups macaroni, cooked
½ cup Italian salad dressing
5 hot dogs, thinly sliced
1 cup celery, diced
¼ cup sweet pickle relish
½ cup sour cream

What to do:
1. In a large bowl, combine macaroni and salad dressing. Refrigerate until cool.
2. Cook hot dogs.
3. Add sliced hot dogs, celery, relish, and sour cream to macaroni.
4. Refrigerate until cool.

Serves 6.

NUTTY
CHICKEN SALAD

You'll need:
2 cups cooked chicken, chopped
1 small onion, chopped
2 stalks celery, chopped
2 teaspoons lemon juice
¾ cup mayonnaise
½ cup toasted almond slivers

What to do:
1. Mix all ingredients.
2. Chill before serving.
Serves 4.

THAT IS ONE NUTTY CHICKEN!

PEA SALAD

You'll need:
- 3 tablespoons mayonnaise
- 3 tablespoons plain yogurt
- 1 small onion, chopped
- 1 package (10 oz.) frozen peas
- 1 cup Cheddar cheese, grated
- 2 cups lettuce, grated

What to do:
1. Combine all ingredients, except lettuce, in bowl. Cover and refrigerate 24 hours.
2. Before serving, add lettuce and mix well.

Serves 6.

RABBIT SALAD

You'll need:
1 cup carrots, grated
1 cup celery, chopped
1 cup apples, chopped
½ cup raisins
¾ cup mayonnaise
½ teaspoon salt

What to do:
1. Combine all ingredients and mix well.
2. Refrigerate until chilled.
3. Serve on lettuce leaves.

Serves 6.

FEED THIS TO YOUR FAVORITE HONEY BUNNY!

SUPER SALAD

You'll need:
1 small head of lettuce
½ cup bacon bits
1 onion, chopped
1 cup mayonnaise
1 jar (2½ oz.) sliced mushrooms, drained

What to do:
1. Tear lettuce into small pieces and put in bottom of a salad bowl.
2. Spread mayonnaise on lettuce.
3. Sprinkle bacon bits, onion, and mushrooms over lettuce.

Serves 6.

SALAD IS GOOD FOOD FOR SUPER HEROES!

BREADS

APPLE BREAD

You'll need:
 2 cups biscuit mix
 ¾ cup sugar
 1 egg
 3 tablespoons oil
 ¾ cup milk
 1 apple, finely chopped

What to do:
 1. Combine biscuit mix and sugar in a large bowl.
 2. In another bowl, combine egg, oil, and milk. Beat well. Stir into biscuit mix and sugar. Mix well.
 3. Stir in apples. Pour into a greased loaf pan.
 4. Bake in a preheated 400°F oven for 35 minutes.

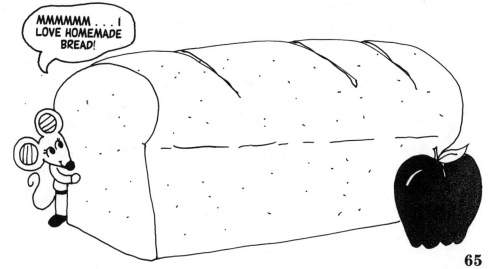

MMMMMM . . . I LOVE HOMEMADE BREAD!

CORN BREAD

You'll need:

2 eggs, beaten
1 cup sour cream
½ cup oil
1½ cups creamed corn
1 cup cornmeal
1 tablespoon baking powder

What to do:

1. Combine eggs, sour cream, oil, and corn in a bowl. Mix well.
2. Stir in cornmeal and baking powder. Mix well.
3. Pour in a greased 8x8-inch baking pan.
4. Bake in a preheated 400°F oven for 35 minutes.

Makes 16 pieces.

GARLIC BREAD

You'll need:
  ½ teaspoon garlic salt
  ½ cup butter, softened
  1 loaf French bread

What to do:
  1. Combine butter and salt. Mix well.
  2. Slice bread into pieces, but not quite all the way through.
  3. Spread butter mixture between slices.
  4. Wrap in aluminum foil. Heat in a preheated 350°F oven for 10 to 12 minutes.

GARLIC BREAD SMELLS TERRIFIC!

ITALIAN BREAD STICKS

You'll need:
  4 hot dog buns
  Italian salad dressing

What to do:
  1. Break the buns in half. Cut each half in half lengthwise.
  2. Put sticks on a cookie sheet. Brush one teaspoon dressing on each stick.
  3. Bake in a preheated 375°F oven for 12 minutes.
Makes 16 servings.

GREAT PARTY FOOD!

LOG CABIN
CINNAMON TOAST

You'll need:
- 2 slices of bread
- 2 teaspoons cinnamon
- 4 teaspoons sugar
- 2 tablespoons butter, melted

What to do:
1. Toast bread and spread one side of each slice with butter.
2. Mix cinnamon and sugar in a cup.
3. Sprinkle each buttered side of toast with cinnamon and sugar.
5. Cut each slice of toast in half. Cut the halves in half. Stack the pieces 2 by 2 as shown in the picture to build a cabin.

Serves 2.

VALENTINE PRETZELS

You'll need:
Frozen bread dough
Poppy or sesame seeds
Salt

What to do:
1. Thaw covered dough overnight in refrigerator, or for several hours at room temperature, until soft enough to shape.
2. On a floured surface, cut dough the long way into 8 strips. Cover and let rest 10 minutes.
3. Roll each strip on floured surface or between floured hands until ½ inch thick and 18 inches long.
4. Cut strips into pieces to shape the letters I LOVE YOU. Shape remaining dough into hearts.
5. Place on a greased cookie sheet.
6. Brush with warm water and sprinkle with poppy or sesame seeds and salt.
7. Let rise, uncovered, for 15 to 20 minutes in warm place.
8. Place a shallow pan of water on bottom shelf of oven before you turn the oven on. Then preheat the oven to 525°F.
9. Bake pretzels on center shelf 15 minutes or until golden brown.

COCOA BROWNIES

You'll need:
- ½ cup margarine, softened
- ¾ cup sugar
- ¼ cup dark corn syrup
- 1 teaspoon vanilla
- 2 eggs
- ½ cup all-purpose flour
- ½ cup unsweetened cocoa powder

What to do:
1. Mix margarine and sugar until smooth.
2. Stir in corn syrup, vanilla, and eggs. Mix well.
3. Stir in flour and cocoa powder. Mix well.
4. Spread in a greased 8x8-inch baking pan.
5. Bake in a preheated 350°F oven for 20 to 25 minutes.

Makes about 16.

I LOVE BROWNIES!

EARTHQUAKE COOKIES

You'll need:
2 cups whipped topping, room temperature
1 egg, beaten
1 teaspoon vanilla
1 box of your favorite cake mix

What to do:
1. Combine whipped topping, egg, and vanilla in a bowl. Mix well.
2. Add cake mix and stir well.
3. Drop by teaspoonfuls on a greased cookie sheet. Bake in a preheated 350°F oven for 15 to 20 minutes.

Makes about 5 dozen.

THESE CAUSE A COMMOTION EVERY TIME I MAKE THEM!

GIANT COOKIES

You'll need:
1 roll refrigerated cookie dough
1 carton ready-spread frosting
Decorator frosting

What to do:
1. Line a cookie sheet with aluminum foil.
2. Cut dough into 36 slices, ¼ inch thick.
3. Place 11 slices in a circle on cookie sheet with the edges touching. Fill in the circle with seven slices.
4. Bake in a preheated 350°F oven for 12 to 15 minutes. When cool, frost and decorate.
5. Repeat steps with remaining slices.

Makes 2 cookies.

THESE GO OVER IN A BIG WAY!

JELLY BEAN COOKIES

You'll need:
   ½ cup butter, softened
   ⅓ cup sugar
   ⅓ cup light brown sugar
   1 egg
   ½ teaspoon baking soda
   ½ teaspoon baking powder
   ½ teaspoon salt
   ½ teaspoon vanilla
   1¼ cups all-purpose flour
   ½ cup rolled oats
   1 cup jelly beans, cut into pieces

What to do:
   1. Mix butter and both sugars until smooth.
   2. Stir in egg, baking soda, baking powder, salt, and vanilla. Mix well.
   3. Stir in flour and oats until well-blended.
   4. Stir in jelly beans.
   5. Drop spoonfuls of batter about 2 inches apart on a greased cookie sheet.
   6. Bake in a preheated 375°F oven for 10 minutes.

Makes about 3 dozen.

FOR KIDS OF ALL AGES!

OATMEAL COOKIES

You'll need:
1 cup butter or margarine, softened
1 cup brown sugar
3 cups rolled oats
1 cup all-purpose flour
1 teaspoon baking soda
1 teaspoon vanilla

What to do:
1. Mix butter and sugar together until smooth.
2. Add remaining ingredients. Mix well.
3. Roll into small balls. Place on a greased cookie sheet several inches apart.
4. Press down until flat.
5. Bake in a preheated 350°F oven for 10 minutes.
Makes about 5 dozen.

OATMEAL COOKIES AND MILK ARE A GREAT AFTERNOON SNACK!

SESAME COOKIES

You'll need:
1½ sticks margarine, softened
1½ cups light brown sugar
1 egg
1 cup all-purpose flour
¼ teaspoon baking powder
1 teaspoon vanilla
¾ cup sesame seeds

What to do:
1. Cream margarine and sugar until smooth.
2. Add egg and mix well.
3. Add remaining ingredients. Mix well.
4. Place teaspoonfuls of dough several inches apart on a greased cookie sheet.
5. Bake in a preheated 300°F oven for 20 minutes.

Makes about 5 dozen.

SUGAR COOKIES

You'll need:
1 stick butter, softened
½ cup sugar
½ cup brown sugar
1 egg, beaten
1½ cups self-rising flour
1 teaspoon vanilla

What to do:
1. Mix butter and both sugars in a bowl until smooth.
2. Add egg and flour. Mix well.
3. Stir in vanilla. Roll dough into a ball and refrigerate overnight.
4. Using a floured rolling pin, roll dough onto a floured surface about ¼-inch thick.
5. Cut into shapes using cookie cutters. Place on a greased cookie sheet.
6. Bake in a preheated 350°F oven for 12 minutes.
7. While cookies are still warm, you can decorate with colored sugar, sparkles, or whatever you like.

Makes about 2½ dozen.

CANDY

CHOCOLATE CRISPIES

You'll need:
1 package (12 oz.) chocolate chips
1 teaspoon butter or margarine
1 can (3 oz.) chow mein noodles

What to do:
1. Heat chocolate and butter or margarine in the top of a double boiler until melted.
2. Remove from heat and stir in noodles.
3. Place teaspoonfuls of mixture on waxed paper. Refrigerate until hard.

Makes about 30.

FUN TO MAKE WITH A FRIEND!

CREAMY FUDGE

You'll need:
2 cups sugar
¾ cup evaporated milk
2 tablespoons butter
½ teaspoon salt
1 package (12 oz.) chocolate chips
1 teaspoon vanilla
2 cups pecans, chopped

What to do:
1. Place sugar, milk, butter, and salt in a pot. Bring to a boil over medium heat, stirring constantly. Boil 2 minutes.
2. Remove from heat. Add chocolate chips, vanilla, and pecans. Stir until chips are melted.
3. Pour into a greased 8x8-inch baking pan. Refrigerate until firm. Cut into squares.

Makes about 16.

CRUNCHIES

You'll need:
- 1 package (12 oz.) semisweet chocolate chips
- 1 can (14 oz.) sweetened condensed milk
- 2 cups crispy rice cereal
- 1 cup peanuts
- 1 teaspoon vanilla

What to do:
1. Melt chocolate chips in a double boiler over low heat.
2. Stir in sweetened condensed milk and remove from heat.
3. Stir in cereal, peanuts, and vanilla. Mix well.
4. Place by teaspoonfuls on waxed paper. Let harden at room temperature for 2 hours.

Makes about 40.

CRUNCHY BUTTERSCOTCH BITS

You'll need:
   1 bag (12 oz.) butterscotch morsels
   3 cups cornflakes, crushed
   1 cup peanuts, chopped

What to do:
   1. Melt butterscotch morsels in a pot over low heat.
   2. Remove from heat. Stir in cornflakes and peanuts un-
      til well mixed.
   3. Place spoonfuls of mixture on waxed paper. Cool be-
      fore serving.
Makes about 30.

FUDGE

You'll need:
   2 (8 oz.) chocolate bars
   3 cups miniature marshmallows
   ¾ cup pecan pieces

What to do:
1. Break chocolate bars into pieces and place in top of a double boiler. Cook over low heat until melted. Stir often.
2. Remove from heat. Stir in marshmallows and nuts.
3. Spread in a greased 8x8-inch baking pan.
4. Refrigerate several hours. Cut into squares.

Makes about 16.

PEANUT BUTTER BALLS

You'll need:
½ cup peanut butter
1 tablespoon jelly
½ cup powdered milk
1 cup branflakes or cornflakes
⅓ cup branflake or cornflake crumbs

What to do:
1. Mix peanut butter and jelly in a bowl.
2. Stir in powdered milk and 1 cup branflakes or corn-flakes. Mix well.
3. Roll mixture into small balls. Roll each ball in crushed flakes.

Makes about 25.

A BIG HIT AT YOUR NEXT TEA PARTY— OR ANYTIME YOU HAVE GUESTS!

DESSERTS

BANANA NUT CAKE

You'll need:
  2 bananas, mashed
  ½ cup chopped pecans
  1 box yellow cake mix
  Frosting

What to do:
  1. Combine bananas, nuts, and dry cake mix.
  2. Prepare mix following directions on cake box.
  3. Spread with your favorite frosting. (We think cara-mel is best!)

GO BANANAS!

CHEESECAKE CUPCAKES

You'll need:
  2 packages (8 oz.) cream cheese, softened
  2 eggs
  1 teaspoon vanilla
  ¾ cup sugar
  Vanilla wafers

What to do:
  1. Combine cream cheese, eggs, vanilla, and sugar in a bowl. Mix well.
  2. Line muffin pan with baking cups. Place a vanilla wafer in each cup.
  3. Fill each cup ¾ full with cream cheese mixture.
  4. Bake in a preheated 350°F oven for 20 minutes.
Makes about 1 dozen.

CHERRY CRUNCH

You'll need:
   1 can (1 lb., 4 oz.) cherry pie filling
   ½ cup nuts, chopped
   ½ box yellow cake mix
   ½ cup butter or margarine

What to do:
   1. Place pie filling in a 10-inch pie pan.
   2. Top with nuts.
   3. Sprinkle cake mix on top.
   4. Dot with butter or margarine.
   5. Bake in a preheated 350°F oven for 25 minutes.

LIFE IS JUST A
BOWL OF CHERRIES!

CHOCOLATE CHEESECAKE CUPCAKES

You'll need:
1 box devil's food cake mix
1 package (8 oz.) cream cheese, softened
1 egg
¾ cup sugar
¾ cup chocolate chips

What to do:
1. Make cake batter using package directions.
2. Place baking cups in muffin pans. Fill cups with cake batter about ⅔ full.
3. Mix cream cheese, egg, sugar, and chocolate chips together.
4. Drop one teaspoonful of cheese mixture on top of each cupcake.
5. Bake following directions on cake mix box.

Makes about 2 dozen.

TREAT SOMEONE WITH CHOCOLATE!

CRAZY CAKE

You'll need:

1½ cups all-purpose flour
1 cup sugar
3 tablespoons cocoa powder
1 teaspoon salt
1 teaspoon baking soda
6 tablespoons vegetable oil
1 tablespoon vinegar
1 teaspoon vanilla
1 cup cold water

EVERYONE GOES CRAZY FOR THIS CAKE!

What to do:

1. Mix flour, sugar, cocoa powder, salt, and soda in a frying pan.
2. Make three holes in the mixture. Place vegetable oil in one hole, vinegar in another, and vanilla in the last one.
3. Pour in water and mix until smooth. Pour in 2 greased and floured cake pans.
4. Bake in a preheated 350°F oven for 25 minutes.

ICING

You'll need:

1½ cups powdered sugar
2 tablespoons cocoa powder
¼ teaspoon salt
3 tablespoons butter, softened
2 tablespoons hot, strong coffee

What to do:

1. Stir together sugar, cocoa powder, and salt. Mix well.
2. Mix with butter and coffee until smooth.
3. Spread on cake.

EASY FRUIT COBBLER

You'll need:
 1 stick butter or margarine, melted
 1 can (16 oz.) fruit cocktail, drained
 1 cup sugar
 1 cup self-rising flour
 2 eggs

What to do:
 1. Pour butter in an 8x8-inch baking pan.
 2. Pour fruit cocktail in pan.
 3. Stir together sugar and flour.
 4. Add eggs and mix well.
 5. Spoon dough over fruit.
 6. Bake in a preheated 300°F oven for 30 minutes.
Serves 8.

THIS SMELLS
WONDERFUL!

ICE CREAM FLOWERPOTS

You'll need:
- 1 pint ice cream, softened
- 4 5-oz. paper cups
- 8 chocolate wafer cookies, finely crumbled
- 2 plastic straws, cut in half
- 4 flowers

What to do:
1. Fill each cup almost to the top with ice cream.
2. Sprinkle the cookie crumbs on top to look like soil.
3. Stick a straw half in the center of each cup. Place cups in freezer.
4. When ready to serve, stick a flower in each straw.

Makes 5.

MAKES US THINK OF SPRING!

KENTUCKY DERBY PIE

You'll need:
  ½ cup all-purpose flour
  1 cup sugar
  ½ cup butter, melted
  1 package (6 oz.) chocolate chips
  2 eggs, slightly beaten
  ¾ cup pecans, chopped
  1 teaspoon vanilla
  1 9-inch pie crust

What to do:
  1. Mix flour and sugar in a bowl. Stir in butter. Mix well.
  2. Stir in chocolate chips, eggs, pecans, and vanilla.
  3. Pour into pie crust.
  4. Bake in a preheated 350°F oven for 1 hour.

LEMON CHESS PIE

You'll need:
  ½ cup butter or margarine
  1½ cups sugar
  1 tablespoon cornstarch
  3 eggs
  2 tablespoons lemon juice
  1 9-inch pie crust

What to do:
  1. Beat butter or margarine and sugar until smooth.
  2. Add other ingredients and mix well.
  3. Pour into pie crust.
  4. Bake 45 to 50 minutes in a preheated 350°F oven.

TAKE A BREAK WITH CHESS PIE!

BEVERAGES

BIRTHDAY PARTY PUNCH

You'll need:
  1 quart orange juice
  1 quart pineapple juice
  1 quart apple juice
  2 quarts ginger ale
  ice or orange or lime sherbet

What to do:
  1. Mix all the juices in a large punch bowl.
  2. Add the ginger ale and ice or sherbet just before serving.
Serves about 30.

HAPPY BIRTHDAY, ROOKIE!

CHOCOLATE PEANUT BUTTER SHAKE

You'll need:
1 pint chocolate chip ice cream
2 tablespoons peanut butter
¼ cup milk
whipped topping
maraschino cherries

What to do:
1. Put ice cream, peanut butter, and milk in a blender. Mix well.
2. Pour in a glass and top with whipped topping and a cherry.
3. Serve with a straw and spoon.

Serves 2.

TREAT YOURSELF AND A FRIEND—OR TWO IF THEY'RE SMALL!

DRACULA'S DELIGHT

You'll need:
3 cups apple juice
4 cups cranberry juice
½ cup lemon juice
1 lemon, sliced
1 cup pineapple bits
1 2-liter bottle ginger ale

What to do:
1. Mix apple juice, cranberry juice, lemon juice, sliced lemon, and pineapple bits in a large container.
2. Refrigerate until chilled.
3. Before serving, add ginger ale and pour into a punch bowl with ice.

Serves 16 to 20.

EGGNOG

You'll need:
    4 eggs, beaten
    2 tablespoons sugar
    2 teaspoons vanilla
    2 teaspoons nutmeg
    4 cups milk

What to do:
1. Mix eggs and sugar in a bowl.
2. Add vanilla and nutmeg. Stir well.
3. Stir in milk.

Serves 4.

HOT COCOA MIX

You'll need:
7 cups powdered milk
1 cup sugar
1½ cups cocoa powder
¼ teaspoon salt
¾ cup dry non-dairy creamer

What to do:
1. Combine all ingredients in a jar and mix well.
2. To make hot cocoa, stir ⅓ cup mixture into 1 cup boiling water.

Makes about 32 servings.

HOW ABOUT SOME HOT COCOA?

SUMMER COOLERS

SHAKE IT UP!

PEANUTTY SHAKE

You'll need:
   1 small banana
   ¼ cup peanut butter
   ½ pint vanilla ice cream
   1 cup milk

What to do:
   1. Place banana and peanut butter in a blender. Mix until smooth.
   2. Slowly add ice cream, then milk. Mix until smooth.
Serves 2.

PINK PARROT

You'll need:
   2 cups cranberry juice
   1 tablespoon lemon juice
   2 scoops orange sherbet

What to do:
   1. Mix juices in a large container.
   2. Pour into 2 tall glasses.
   3. Top with a scoop of sherbet.
Serves 2.

SUN TEA

You'll need:
  1 quart water
  2 tea bags

What to do:
  1. Place water and tea in a large, covered glass jar.
  2. Set in the sun for 3 hours.
  3. Serve with ice and orange or lemon slices.

PERFECT FOR THOSE
DAYS WHEN YOU
HAVE SO MUCH MORE
TO DO!

MICROWAVE DISHES

MANY KIDS ARE COOKING IN MICROWAVE OVENS.

BACON

You'll need:
  6 slices bacon

What to do:
  1. Place bacon slices side-by-side on several paper towels.
  2. Cover with a paper towel.
  3. Microwave on HIGH for 6 to 8 minutes or until crisp.
  4. Let stand several minutes before serving.

BAKED POTATO

What to do:
1. Wash and scrub potatoes.
2. Prick each potato with a fork in several places.
3. Place in microwave with about 1 inch between each potato.
4. Microwave on HIGH. Cooking times:

   1 potato—5 minutes

   2 potatoes—7 minutes

   4 potatoes—14 minutes

Times may vary.

Turn the potatoes over halfway through cooking time.

Let stand 5 minutes before serving.

ANYONE CAN BE A GOOD CHEF WITH THIS EASY RECIPE!

BEANS AND FRANKS

You'll need:
½ onion, chopped
2 cans (10 oz.) bean with bacon soup
1 can (15 oz.) kidney beans
4 hot dogs, sliced

What to do:
1. Place onion in a 3-quart, microwave-safe casserole dish. Cover and microwave on HIGH 3 minutes. Stir after 1½ minutes.
2. Stir in remaining ingredients. Cover and microwave on HIGH 10 minutes. Stir at 3 and 6 minutes.
3. Remove from oven. Let stand 5 minutes before serving.

Serves 6.

BEANS AND FRANKS ARE A FUN LUNCH!

CHICKEN

Place chicken on a microwave-safe dish with meatiest part toward the edge. Cover. Microwave on HIGH. Let stand 5 minutes before serving.

AMOUNT   COOKING TIME
1 piece—4 to 6 minutes
2 pieces—6 to 7½ minutes
3 pieces—7½ to 9 minutes
4 pieces—9 to 10½ minutes
6 pieces—17 to 20 minutes

If cooking more than 3 pieces, move halfway through cooking time.

COOL OR HOT CARROTS

You'll need:
2 pounds carrots, thinly sliced
¼ cup water
1 can (10 oz.) tomato soup
½ cup vinegar
¼ cup vegetable oil
¼ cup sugar
1 teaspoon dry mustard
2 teaspoons Worcestershire sauce
½ onion, chopped

What to do:
1. Place carrots and water in a 3-quart microwave-safe casserole. Cover and microwave on HIGH for 10 minutes. Stir at 3 and 6 minutes.
2. Remove from oven and drain.
3. In a large bowl, combine remaining ingredients. Mix well.
4. Stir in carrots.
5. Cover and refrigerate 4 hours.

This can be served either hot or cold. To make as a hot dish, cook the carrots as directed. Add 2 tablespoons of margarine and one can of soup. Cover and microwave on HIGH for 1½ minutes or until warm.
Serves 10.

CARROTS ARE GOOD-FOR-YOU FOOD!

CORN ON THE COB

What to do:

1. Place the unhusked corn in a microwave-safe dish. Cover.
2. Cook on HIGH for 3 minutes for each ear. Let stand several minutes before removing from oven.
3. Ask an adult using pot holders or cooking mitts to carefully remove the husks. The corn will be very hot!

BE VERY CAREFUL— THIS IS HOT CORN!

CRUMBY CHICKEN

You'll need:
1 egg
¼ cup margarine, melted
1 teaspoon seasoned salt
1 cup soda cracker crumbs
4 chicken breasts

What to do:
1. Combine egg, margarine, and salt in a bowl.
2. Place cracker crumbs in another bowl.
3. Roll chicken in crumbs then dip in egg mixture. Roll in crumbs again.
4. Place chicken in an 8x8-inch baking dish. Cover with waxed paper. Microwave on HIGH 18 to 22 minutes. Move a half turn after 10 minutes.

Serves 4.

GREAT CHICKEN DINNER!

HAMBURGERS

You'll need:
2 hamburger patties, ½-inch thick

What to do:
1. Line a microwave-safe plate with several paper towels. Place patties on top. Cover with a paper towel or waxed paper.
2. Microwave on HIGH for 1½ to 2 minutes.
3. Turn patties over. Microwave second side for 1½ to 2 minutes.
4. Let stand for 3 minutes before serving.

HOT DOGS

Place hot dogs on a microwave-safe plate or bowl. Pierce skin with a fork or knife. Cover with waxed paper. If microwaving in a bun, wrap in a paper towel. Microwave on HIGH.

NUMBER	TIME
1	1 minute
2	1 to 2 minutes
4	3 to 4 minutes
6	4 to 5 minutes. Place in ½ cup water. Rearrange after 2 minutes.
10	7 to 9 minutes. Place in ¾ cup water. Rearrange after 4 minutes.

ITALIAN MEATBALLS

You'll need:
1 pound ground beef
½ cup dry Italian bread crumbs
¼ cup milk
½ onion, finely chopped
1 egg
2 teaspoons Worcestershire sauce
¼ teaspoon salt

What to do:
1. Combine all ingredients in a bowl and mix well.
2. Shape into balls about 1½ inches in size.
3. Place meatballs in an 8x8-inch microwave-safe baking dish.
4. Cover loosely and microwave on HIGH for 3 minutes.
5. Rearrange meatballs. Microwave another 6 minutes.
6. Let stand 3 minutes. Drain.

Makes about 24.

THESE MEATBALLS ARE GREAT OVER SPAGHETTI NOODLES!

MACARONI AND CHEESE

You'll need:
  1 can (10 oz.) Cheddar cheese soup
  ¾ cup milk
  1½ cups Cheddar cheese, grated
  3 cups elbow macaroni, cooked

What to do:
  1. In a 2-quart microwave-safe casserole, stir soup and milk until blended.
  2. Stir in cheese and macaroni.
  3. Cover and microwave on HIGH for 10 minutes. Stir at 3 and 6 minutes.
  4. Remove and let stand 5 minutes before serving.
Serves 6.

MINT CHOCOLATE CAKE

You'll need:
2 cups dry chocolate cake mix
1 egg
½ teaspoon vanilla
⅓ cup oil
¾ cup water
½ cup mint chocolate chips

What to do:
1. Combine all ingredients, except chips, in a large bowl. Mix until smooth.
2. Pour into an 8x8-inch microwave-safe baking dish.
3. Sprinkle chocolate chips on top.
4. Microwave on HIGH 7 to 9 minutes.

MAKES A BEAUTIFUL BIRTHDAY CAKE!

NACHOS

You'll need:
  1 bag (11 oz.) tortilla chips
  2 cups Cheddar cheese, grated
  Salsa

What to do:
  1. Place tortilla chips in a microwave-safe bowl.
  2. Sprinkle cheese on top.
  3. Microwave on HIGH 1 minute or until cheese is
     melted.
  4. Top with salsa before serving.

WE ALL LOVE
MEXICAN FOOD!

ONION POPCORN

You'll need:
1 stick margarine
1 envelope (1¼ oz.) onion soup mix
4 quarts popped popcorn

What to do:
1. Place margarine in a 4-cup glass measuring cup. Cover and microwave on HIGH for 45 seconds or until melted.
2. Remove from oven and stir in soup mix.
3. Place popcorn in a large bowl. Pour butter mixture on top and mix well.

I LOVE TO EAT POPCORN AND WATCH OLD MOVIES!

PEANUT BUTTER FUDGE

You'll need:
1 can (14 oz.) sweetened condensed milk
2 cups peanut butter chips
1 ounce unsweetened chocolate
1 teaspoon vanilla
1 cup peanuts

What to do:
1. Place milk, peanut butter chips, and chocolate in a 2-quart microwave-safe casserole.
2. Microwave on HIGH for 1 minute.
3. Stir and microwave another 3 minutes or until chocolate is melted.
4. Stir in vanilla and nuts.
5. Pour into a greased 8x8-inch baking dish.
6. Refrigerate until firm. Cut into squares.

Makes about 16 pieces.

FUDGE IS OUR FAVORITE TREAT!

PIZZA

You'll need:
1 English muffin
2 tablespoons pizza sauce
2 slices mozzarella cheese
Your favorite pizza toppings

What to do:
1. Spread 1 tablespoon pizza sauce on each muffin half.
2. Place cheese and other toppings on top.
3. Place on a paper towel or microwave-safe plate.
4. Microwave on HIGH for 2 minutes.

PUDDING

You'll need:
1 package (3½ oz.) pudding mix
2 cups milk

What to do:
1. Pour pudding mix in a 1-quart glass casserole or measuring cup.
2. Add enough milk to dissolve pudding.
3. Stir in remaining milk.
4. Microwave on HIGH 6½ to 7½ minutes or until pudding boils. Stir after 2 and 4 minutes.

Pudding will become thicker as it cools.

Serves 4.

YUMMM . . . PUDDING!

SCALLOPED POTATOES

You'll need:
¾ cup milk
1 can (10 oz.) cream of mushroom soup
4 medium potatoes, sliced about ⅛ inch thick
1 cup Cheddar cheese, grated
½ small onion, chopped

What to do:
1. Combine milk and soup in a microwave-safe 2-quart casserole.
2. Stir in remaining ingredients.
3. Cover and microwave on HIGH for 10 minutes.
3. Stir and microwave another 12 minutes or until potatoes are tender.

Serves 8.

SCALLOPED POTATOES ARE A GREAT SIDE DISH!

SCRAMBLED EGGS

You'll need:
  2 eggs
  ⅛ cup milk
  Dash of salt and pepper

What to do:
  1. Place all ingredients in a glass measuring cup or microwave-safe bowl. Beat until well-mixed.
  2. Microwave on HIGH 2 to 3 minutes, or until fluffy but still moist. Stir every minute.

TASTY TOMATOES

You'll need:
- 4 tomatoes
- 2 teaspoons dried onion
- 4 teaspoons sugar
- ½ teaspoon pepper
- 1 cup Cheddar cheese, grated
- 1 cup potato chips, crushed

What to do:
1. Cut tomatoes in half and place on a microwave-safe plate.
2. Combine remaining ingredients in a bowl. Sprinkle on tomato halves.
3. Microwave on HIGH for 5 to 6 minutes. Move a half turn halfway through cooking.

ESPECIALLY GOOD WITH HOMEGROWN TOMATOES!

TEXAS TRASH

You'll need:
1 stick margarine
2 tablespoons Worcestershire sauce
1 teaspoon seasoned salt
2 cups pretzel bits
2 cups wheat cereal
2 cups corn cereal
1 cup mixed nuts

What to do:
1. Place margarine in a microwave-safe casserole. Microwave on HIGH for 1 minute or until melted.
2. Stir in Worcestershire sauce and seasoned salt.
3. Add pretzel bits and cereals. Mix well.
4. Microwave on HIGH for 6 minutes. Stir at 3 minutes.
5. Add nuts and mix well.
6. Let stand 10 minutes before serving.

SERVE TEXAS TRASH AT YOUR NEXT HOEDOWN!

VEGGIES AND CHICKEN

You'll need:
1 bag (1-pound) frozen mixed vegetables
4 chicken breasts
¼ cup mustard
1 can (2.8 oz.) French fried onions

What to do:
1. Place vegetables in a 12x8-inch microwave-safe baking dish. Cover with plastic wrap and microwave on HIGH for 3 minutes.
2. Place chicken on vegetables. Spread mustard on top of meat.
3. Sprinkle with French fried onions.
4. Cover with wax paper. Microwave on HIGH 18 minutes. Rotate ½ turn after 9 minutes. Let stand 5 minutes before serving.

Serves 4.

INDEX

BREADS

COOKIES

CANDY

DESSERTS

BEVERAGES

MICROWAVE DISHES